6 EASY STEPS TO CUSTOMIZE A STYLE GUIDE: WHAT'S YOUR STYLE?

ROBIN MARTIN

THE-EFA.ORG

Copyright © 2017, 2020 Robin Martin
Cover and design © 2020 Editorial Freelancers Association
New York, NY

All rights reserved.
No part of this publication may be reproduced, distributed, or transmitted in any form or by any means, including, but not limited to, photocopying, recording, or other electronic or mechanical methods, without the prior written permission of the publisher, except in the case of brief quotations embodied in critical reviews and certain other noncommercial uses permitted by copyright law. For permission requests, write to the publisher at "Attention: Publications Chairperson," at the address below.

266 West 37th St. 20th Floor
New York, NY 10018
office@the-efa.org

ISBN paperback: 978-1-880407-42-4
ISBN ebook: 978-1-880407-43-1

Martin, Robin. *6 Easy Steps to Customize a Style Guide: What's Your Style?*

Originally published in a slightly different version titled *What's Your Style? Customize a Style Guide in Six Easy Steps* in 2017 by Robin Martin and The Editorial Freelancers Association (EFA).

Published in the United States of America by the Editorial Freelancers Association.
Subject Categories: Editing & Proofreading | Communication Studies | Business Skills

Legal Disclaimer
While the publisher and author have made every attempt to verify that the information provided in this book is correct and up to date, the publisher and author assume no responsibility for any error, inaccuracy, or omission.

The advice, examples, and strategies contained herein are not suitable for every situation. Neither the publisher nor author shall be liable for damages arising therefrom. This book is not intended for use as a source of legal or financial advice. Running a business involves complex legal and financial issues. You should always retain competent legal and financial professionals to provide guidance.

EFA Publications Director: Robin Martin
Copyeditor: Amy Spungen
Proofreader: Christi Cervetti
Book Designer: Kevin Callahan | BNGO Books
Cover Designer: Ann Marie Manca

"In matters of style, swim with the current; in matters of principle, stand like a rock."

~ Thomas Jefferson

Contents

Introduction	vii
Part One: Background Basics	1
Part Two: The Six Steps—an Overview	5
Part Three: Breakdown	7
Notes	21
About the Editorial Freelancers Association (EFA)	23

Introduction

I'd be lying if I didn't say up front that writing a manual for editors is nerve-racking. Now, make that a manual about style guidelines, and I fear I've really stepped into some dangerous territory. Not a week goes by where a question related to style doesn't get thoroughly worked through in the Editorial Freelancers Association (EFA) members-only Discussion List, and often there are several points contended! I have read those discussions and I want to acknowledge right up front that some of you may already have a different way to customize style guides. And without a doubt, you have a preference for certain elements of grammar, usage, and even typography over others, and you have more than a few pet peeves when it comes to these things.

Most competent editors these days have moved beyond the reputation that once preceded those in this profession, one left over perhaps from having a paper "bled on" by an English teacher wielding a red pen, that we are "inflexible." (Though many of us do see ourselves as caretakers of language, and sometimes we get accused of being bullies or snobs or grammar police.) It is true, we have our strong opinions based on what we have learned, and sometimes our guardianship borders on dogma. In the words of Associated Press (AP) former president and CEO Louis D. Boccardi, "Journalists approach these style questions with varying degrees of passion."[1]

For my purposes here, I won't suggest that some style choices are superior to others, and neither will I suggest that any one editor must be an expert at multiple styles. I do, however, feel it's a no-brainer that we must have at least a working knowledge of, and access to, a number of existing style guides for reference. As freelancers, any time we take on a new client or project, we have to assess the standard for the particular rhetorical situation and adapt to the needs of the client and their readers. If we are not comfortable with our skills in any one style and are not willing to put the time in to study our resources, we ought to pass the work on to a colleague who is. Customizing a style guide should never be used as a lazy excuse not to use an existing one when the situation calls for it.

That said, adhering strictly to any single style guide is often unfavorable, impossible, or inappropriate. Maintaining consistent style throughout the course of a project, however, is a crucial element of any editorial work, whether you are copyediting the main body of a manuscript, front and back material, charts and tables, or design elements. Sometimes it is necessary to finesse the rules. It has been said, "Punctuation is there to serve the writing, not the other way around." And though style is much more than punctuation, this idea, the premise that style should serve substance, is why I have written this booklet.

I have eleven years' experience customizing style guides as a freelancer and as the managing editor of a literary magazine. One of my more recent projects was as a volunteer right here at the EFA, collaborating with other stakeholders to generate a house style for our organization. I have taught MLA, AP, and CMOS styles to students, and I work with each of these style guides online as well as in print.

I have found that a handful of core best practices carry over from one project to the next and make customization of style guides quite simple. I hope you find my six-step approach, presented here, easy and useful.

Part One: Background Basics

Popular Style Guides

There are a handful of common style guides designed to suit the fields in which they are used. The one that most Americans are introduced to first is that of the Modern Language Association (MLA), commonly used in high schools and liberal arts institutions. The *MLA Handbook* originated in 1951, when the executive director of the MLA set out to create a simpler way to prepare a manuscript for publication. The resulting *MLA Style Sheet* attempted to settle arguments among MLA scholars. According to Phyllis Franklin, the MLA's executive director in July 2002—when the sixth edition of the handbook was published—the style sheet "codified uniform practices among journal editors and university presses." It has become the standard for secondary and liberal arts undergraduate students.[2]

The *Publication Manual of the American Psychological Association* (APA), often introduced to academics in college social science, engineering, and business classes, first came about in 1929, when editors of psychological journals met and created a set of instructions and procedures intended to make manuscript preparation more cost-effective and communication of scientific principles clearer.[3] The manual has been revised and expanded many times.

The *American Medical Association Manual of Style* (AMA) first appeared in 1962. Now in its eleventh edition, it was created to impose a set of rules for in-house staff of the AMA's scientific journals. As the standard style for medical journalism, AMA contains nearly 250 pages of nomenclature and an extensive chapter on legal and ethical considerations, as is appropriate for the field.[4]

The Associated Press Stylebook (AP) was designed for journalists and newspaper editors in 1975. Boccardi writes, "The orders were: Make clear and simple rules, permit few exceptions to the rules, and rely heavily on the chosen dictionary as the arbiter of conflicts."[5] The AP style guide, used by major news outlets, was created to streamline the printing process and is most famously (infamously, in some circles!) rumored to have been responsible for the elimination of the serial comma in an effort to increase the space available for "more important" characters.

The last one I will mention is *The Chicago Manual of Style* (CMOS), which originated in the composing room of the University of Chicago Press at the end of the nineteenth century as one of the first published standardizations of typographical style. It has grown and expanded through seventeen editions and is now widely used in trade publishing and academics. One reason it may be preferred is that CMOS does allow for — and, in fact, is friendly to — adaptation.[6] This is why I will focus on it for the purposes of this booklet.

What is House Style?

A publishing house, journalism outlet, corporation, sole proprietor, or the like, wanting to assure consistency in their brand and writerly voice, maintains a house style guide reflecting their official grammatical, mechanical, usage, and design preferences for the writing they produce.

EFA member Katharine O'Moore-Klopf explains style sheets on her website, KOKedit.com:

> There are a good many things that a copyeditor must keep track of in a manuscript to ensure that the finished book or article is consistent throughout and doesn't jar the reader by odd deviations from its intended structure, message, or voice.

What's Your Style?

What are some of these? Proper spelling and capitalization of jargon, for a start. There's much more, such as chronological numbering of chapters and references, physical and personality traits of fictional characters, and how ranges of numbers are handled.

To document choices about such items, a copyeditor creates a style sheet for each manuscript. It then serves as a reference for anyone who deals with the manuscript later in the process, including the author, the proofreader, the production editor, and the indexer.[7]

There is plenty of room for preferences in written English language. As long as the choices made are used consistently, they need not necessarily be called errors. Of course, there are some things that are just plain wrong and not open for debate (like how to punctuate a contraction or the definition and spelling of many words). But just as speakers of English may have a talent for code switching or expressing themselves verbally in different ways befitting various situations, writers of English may do the same thing.

In a post on the EFA Discussion List not too long ago, member Cheryl Murphy (Ink Slinger Editorial Services) put it this way:

> Developing your own style is a good thing. But there's a difference between choosing to ignore errors and having valid reasons for style deviations. People use style guides because they are standardized. We make tweaks to those standards to create our own house style, but those tweaks are based on balancing CMOS and craft.[8]

Rules of grammar and usage may be prescriptive or descriptive, and there are differences among reference books, dictionaries, and other respectable sources. As I explained in the introduction, it isn't my intention to elevate one over another or to suggest an open disregard, only to recommend approaching style with an open mind. As former *Chicago Manual of Style Online* Q&A editor Carol Fisher Saller writes in the introduction of her book *The Subversive Copy Editor*:

> To live a good life as a copy editor, a person must occasionally think outside the rules. To copy edit is to confront and solve an

endless series of problems great and small. . . . A need to always cleave to the rules can be counterproductive. . . . It's not a matter of being correct or incorrect. It's only a style.[9]

I recommend reading Saller's book, now in an expanded second edition, if you object to the idea of customizing a style guide for practicality, convenience, or readability. This book is an excellent one, arguing for the customization of style guides and for holstering the weapons of dogmatic grammar police.

I presume not only the freedom to customize, but the obligation to customize. A consistent house style is a kind of contract with the reader, designed with them in mind.

Part Two: The Six Steps — an Overview

Step 1. Establish Rhetorical Situation

The prep work starts with asking the question, "Does this project come with a built-in style guide preference?" The answer is dependent on the many factors of the rhetorical situation and will create the foundation on which the project's style guide will be built.

Step 2. Identify and Map Patterns

By identify and map patterns, I mean look at the source material and supporting documents to see what patterns the writing contains and track them. This will often reveal preferences in handling specific terminology (to hyphenate, to capitalize, to italicize, to use all caps), particular elements of voice, etc. This takes place during the first read-through.

Step 3. Query

The writer and the editor must be seen as partners, not adversaries, in the process of bringing the writing to its audience. Querying is the step where I present options to the writer with examples, and I am available to answer their questions.

Step 4. Structure and Format

There are many ways to present a customized style guide. It could be anything from an email or a one-pager to a chart or a manual. It might be loosely organized or extremely formal. It might live in an online database or a print document. It might be alphabetized and cross-referenced or organized according to topic.

Step 5. Apply

During subsequent reads, while copyediting, I continue to reference the guide I have created, applying its custom style.

Step 6. Adjust and Refine

Based on feedback from the writer, typesetters, subsequent readers, and editors, I adjust the style guide as appropriate. There is nothing that says once a guide is created it is set in stone. In fact, just like the English language itself, style can be alive and breathing.

Part Three:
Breakdown

1. Establish Rhetorical Situation

When I receive a document for copyediting, I ask the writer a simple question: "Did you follow any particular style guide regarding usage and mechanics as you wrote this?" I ask if they have an established house style guide to share with me. Often, this isn't something writers have even considered, but it is the first step in establishing a collaborative relationship with them. They may not know what the standard style guide for the industry, association, publisher, or platform is, or even that such a thing exists. In that case, it will be up to me to find out and answer that question for them. I need to start by learning more about the writer, the audience, the setting, and the purpose. In other words, I need to understand the rhetorical situation.

The Online Writing Lab (OWL) at Purdue defines rhetorical situations this way:

> There is no singular rhetorical situation that applies to all instances of communication. Rather, all human efforts to communicate occur within innumerable individual rhetorical situations that are particular to those specific moments of communication. . . . Each individual rhetorical situation shares five basic elements with all other rhetorical situations:
> 1. A text (i.e., an actual instance or piece of communication)
> 2. An author (i.e., someone who uses communication)

3. An audience (i.e., a recipient of communication)
4. Purposes (i.e., the varied reasons both authors and audiences communicate)
5. A setting (i.e., the time, place, and environment surrounding a moment of communication).[10]

For more about how to determine a rhetorical situation, I recommend the OWL resource.

With information about the rhetorical situation in hand, I can look at historical documents, go to the publisher or university's website, and use my own experience as an expert in that subject area to determine the best basic style guide to follow. By historical documents, I mean: If this is a booklet in a series, how have other booklets been styled? If it is an article in a magazine, what styles do they prefer? If it is a novel for self-publishing, what do similar novels in the bookstore use? If it is content for a website, but they don't specify a style guide, can I find patterns and preferences in the previously published content?

What will work best for the audience and the genre? Who is going to ultimately be reading this book? I look into whether one style is more "right" than another, so I can approach the manuscript keeping one base style guide in mind. Often, as the resident expert, I can just select one style and apply it consistently throughout. If it is being submitted to a publisher, what does their submission policy say regarding style? If the project has a publisher with clearly defined style guidelines, such as the *Journal of the American Medical Association* (JAMA), the US State Department, or *The New Yorker*, my role as an editor is simpler: Customize at my own peril, and don't ask why. Accept these internal style guidelines, and make them my own for the duration.

The three scenarios that follow are fictionalized amalgams of my actual clients and experiences.

Scenario #1 AIMEE

Aimee is a public speaker who has seen promising success on the local motivational speakers circuit. She is hoping to extend her reach by self-publishing a nonfiction manuscript to sell at the back of the room after her presentations. Aimee knows nothing about writing conventions, but her audience, mostly young people not yet established along a career path, loves her style. She has hired me as a copyeditor for her project.

Scenario #2 MARLA'S LITERARY MAGAZINE
Marla, a former journalist, comes from commercial publishing and has just purchased a floundering artsy literary magazine. As the new executive editor/publisher, she plans to institute a more professional image for the magazine to make it successful. She has some definite preferences for styles she wants to incorporate, and none of them precisely fit any preexisting style guide. She has hired me as managing editor for the magazine. The target audience for her magazine is older adults with disposable income.

Scenario #3 COOKBOOK FOR THE COOKWELL TEAM
Created by a group of chefs as support material for the launch of an innovative cooking tool, much of the style has been established by a well-respected branding and promotional team for an audience of young-adult to middle-aged households. The website has been set up. The labels and logos are designed and printed. The tagline is established, and it uses headline style capitalization and end punctuation, even though it is a sentence fragment. I am tasked to smooth transitions between voices and authors so the recipes all appear to come from one author: the brand.

2. Identify and Map Patterns

Writers and editors love to argue about issues of style. This is clear from reading the EFA's Discussion List, where weekly there is some colorful discussion about rules, and also from reading just about any forum for writers and editors. On the *Writer's Digest* magazine website, for example, former online manager Brian A. Klems responds to questions such as this one:

> Q: In my writing I strictly follow the rules in *The Chicago Manual of Style*. For example, in a sentence joined with an "and," I place a comma after the last word before the "and" when the first part of the sentence is a complete sentence. I have

received a rejection with the first page sent back and the editor's deletion marks are in contradiction to the rule in the *Chicago Manual*. Should I follow the *Chicago Manual* in my fiction writing or not?

–Carolyn Boyles

A: According to *Formatting & Submitting Your Manuscript* (and editors I've spoken to at conferences), most book publishers use *The Chicago Manual of Style*—or some variation of it—as a formatting guide for their books. . . .

The key to writing any manuscript is to be consistent—in other words, no matter what style you are using (Chicago, AP-style, your sixth-grade English teacher's rulebook), stick with it. Publishers and editors tend to be forgiving when reading a manuscript that doesn't embrace their style, but are less forgiving when the formatting is all over the place (e.g., using a comma in a parallel sentence structure sometimes and not using it other times; italicizing book titles in the first few chapters but underlining it [in] others). This lack of consistency looks unprofessional and lazy—two traits that could potentially cost you a deal. To a writer it may seem like nitpicking, but to an editor it shows discipline and an author who values the craft.

Most magazine and newspaper publishers, on the other hand, use *The Associated Press Stylebook and Libel Manual* as a guide for their publications. Although many, like *Writer's Digest*, take a few liberties with it to fit their own particular house styles. So don't read too much into style edits.

It's probably wise for all writers to have both the *Chicago Manual* and the *AP Stylebook* on their bookshelves—along with maybe a good luck charm.[11]

I take these things away from Klems's response: It is important to be both consistent and flexible when editing and customizing style, and **the publisher's house style prevails**.

So once I have completed step one, I have a basic understanding of whose rules we are following; then during the first reading, I can isolate patterns of error—or nonconformity with that style—in the manuscript. I often make notes at this stage that only I can understand. I try to remember to write the page numbers where questionable items appear. This makes it easier to refer back to them later.

Another thing I note in a manuscript, when appropriate, is whether the writer has used offensive or divisive words or phrases, and if so, whether they have done this intentionally. I believe that because we need to be the change we hope to see in the world, it is worth it to note terminology or phrasing that is potentially sexist or racist or otherwise exclusionary, and—without judgment—check in with the writer to determine that they have used this language intentionally. A great resource, for anyone interested in learning more about this idea, is Karen Yin's *Conscious Style Guide*. Even CMOS seventeenth edition has adopted the pronoun *they* as an acceptable gender-neutral alternative to the awkward and outdated *he/she*.[12]

Scenario #1: Remember, Aimee is self-publishing. She is the publisher, and no one knows her subject or her audience better than she does. In email correspondence, Aimee has a habit of using all caps for emphasis. Though she has apologized for "yelling," she is emphatic that this is just part of who she is. Reading through Aimee's manuscript, I realize that this practice has carried over to her book. So I take a look at her previously released promotional material, and guess what? ALL CAPS. I go to YouTube to watch a few of her video clips and find that she is animated and generous with her hand gestures. Also, in a separate issue, the way she writes internal dialogue varies from one place to the next—sometimes it is indicated by italics, and sometimes it is in double quotation marks, single quotation marks, or even block formatting.

In the first case, I can take a clue from Aimee; let's keep some caps. Although I may want to suggest she use fewer, or that she use them consistently, if she doesn't want to give them up completely I will defer. After all, she is the publisher. In the second case, with the internal dialogue, I am the resident expert and can suggest one style. I see this much like fixing a spelling error. In either case, I will present these style decisions to Aimee so she can see I have been intentional and careful, and also to give her an opportunity to let me know if she has a different idea.

Scenario #2: Though Marla is the publisher, her desire to present a professional image might trump any quirky things she might add to basic CMOS guidelines. As the new managing editor, it is my job to be the CMOS expert and, especially for the first few issues, query Marla about styles for which CMOS is ambiguous or in opposition to her common practices. Because Marla worked at another publication before buying this one, I can look at past issues for clues as to where she might want to deviate from CMOS. Because she will always write the editor's letter for the front of the magazine, I can ask her about any inconsistency that appears in her writing before changing it. For instance: Serial comma or no serial comma? I notice Marla does not use serial commas in her writing, no doubt a holdover from her newspaper days. Does she want me to add them? Perhaps only when the meaning is ambiguous? For this, I have to query.

Scenario #3: The Cookwell Team, as a corporation, will be the publisher of this cookbook, and this group of chefs have trusted the branding/PR company to utilize best practices for selling to their target audience. The decision to use headline style and end punctuation for their sentence fragment logo, for instance, has been accepted, and I must also accept it as part of their style. I can look at the website content to discover the predominant voice and make notes about styles already in use on the site.

As I make my first pass through the cookbook, I'll take notes about variations in voice and elements of style. Is there anything all writers do consistently that we want to implement? They are chefs, after all — they may have read a cookbook or two. I like to be open to the possibility that a choice that might look odd to me may have been an intentional move by the writer based on something they know that I don't.

Do all of the writers on the team use abbreviations for measurements? There are many ways to indicate that they mean "the big spoon" — T, Tbs, tbs, or tablespoon. As a general rule, one alternative is not more right than another; there just has to be consistency. Also, I'll have to see how the instructions are written: Are they complete sentences? Paragraphs or bullets? Do they have end punctuation? Are they written verb first? Once I gather the info, then I can use my professional judgment and present options to the team for their input.

Here are two examples of what my notes might look like at this stage:

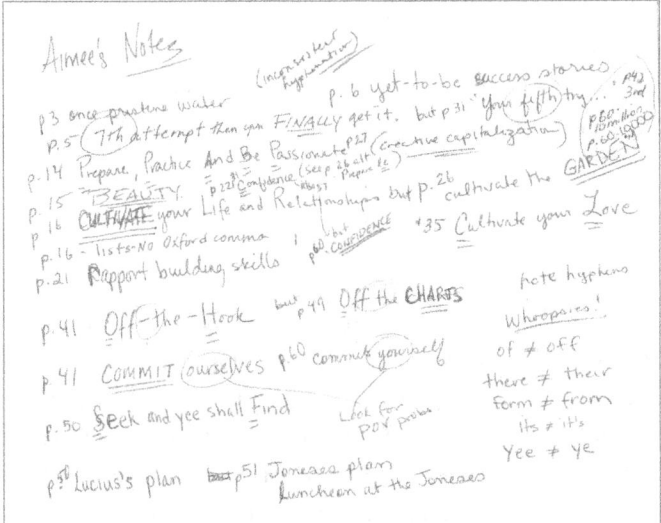

Figure i. Handwritten notes (Scenario #1: Aimee)

Marla's Magazine NOTES

Will use Chicago Manual of Style primarily.

an old 45 record p. 2 (number) ?

Semicolons & colons capitalization following colon? See p. 2, 3, 7, 8

Note Marla's request for light to no Scare Quotation marks: See page 3, 40.

commonly confused words. Like poring vs pouring (p 3)

Hyphen use with modification and numbers, in particular. A three-year old (p 2, column 1) a three-year-old (p 3, column 2).

150 feet away (p 10)

Prolific em dash as an alternative to parentheses, commas, or a colon. Look for too many! Alternate with paren/comma. Check for unintentional en dash or hyphen- see p. 12, 42

Cabernet Sauvignon, pinot gris?

Punctuation in relation to closing quotation marks? See p. 13, 23, 24.

towards v *toward*

til or *'til* as short word for *until*?

Album Titles? Song Titles ?

Titles of movies and of television and radio programs? The names of broadcast networks, channels?

The Latin names of species of plants and animals?

"in my twenties" p. 33

"This was the nineties" p. 36

#3 bus

Peeled vs pealed (p 30)

o'clock- page 5

The meeting continued until half past three. P 37

The first train leaves at 5:22 a.m. and the last at 11:00 p.m.

She was awake at 3:00 PM – check with Marla for time style

Charlie, next to me, repeats over and over in his Oklahoma drawl, "M***$*ers," which comes out, "Muh$**ers."

a quarter after five – page 30

Figure ii. Typewritten notes (Scenario #2: Marla)

The last piece of step two is to draft a list of style options and questions for the writer.

3. Query

Laurel Ferejohn is an EFA member and frequent Discussion List contributor. On her website, laurelferejohn.com, she defines effective queries: "Effective queries go straight to the problem and draw helpful responses, and there is nothing like this kind of exchange to buoy the confidence—and the trust—of both parties. Go for CUSP queries: concise, unambiguous, specific, polite."[13]

Former CMOS editor Saller says when we query we should aim for "carefulness, transparency, and flexibility."[14] So before I reach out to the writer, I understand the benefits of one option over another and have the base style guide at the ready to reference. I know what patterns they seem to prefer, because I have been through their manuscript and taken notes. I know how well they understand, and whether or not they care about, these language issues, and how much autonomy they have given me.

For Scenario #3, my query to the writers might look like this:

> *I notice that some of the recipes in your cookbook spell out terms and others abbreviate terms. For example, in Recipe A, you call for 1 C flour and 1 cup sugar. Also, you have different capitalization and hyphenation practices: In Recipe B, you use a lowercase c to indicate a cup, and in another you hyphenate 1-cup. Do you have a preference for this and/or other terms frequently found in recipes? Is there a particular cookbook you would like to emulate?*

In Scenario #2, Marla is building her own style for the magazine based on CMOS but with her own preferences; it is up to us to establish what is the "right" style. And Marla is an editorial professional. So my query to Marla about the serial comma might look like this:

> *Serial/Oxford comma: Yea or Nay?*

I don't need to overexplain. I don't need to bring my own biases into it—not unless she says it is my decision. (I have my biases and opinions like everyone else, so if she asks me? Yay Oxford.)

In Scenario #1, Aimee has a reference to "a late night meeting: It was 2 AM in fact." Later, she references a "twenty-two caliber weapon," and still later, she says one event begins at 1 pm and another at 2:00pm. I wouldn't bother Aimee with details and explanations either; she will trust me to find the one appropriate style and implement it consistently throughout. Then I'll just let her know about the change.

But should those same things arise with Marla's editor's letter, I'd add something like this:

CMOS 9.2, 9.38, and 9.19 all provide guidance, but there are so many special cases and exceptions that I thought I'd check in and see what you prefer for our house style.

If I gave that to Aimee, she'd be confused and maybe even irritated. Rhetorical situations apply for correspondence with the client as well!

4. Structure and Format

After querying the writer and resolving any questions we have about issues in the manuscript, having determined what we will consistently use throughout the project, then it is time to build the house style document. Deciding on this structure should not be difficult. The primary considerations are related to the rhetorical situation that has been established in the first step of this process: One, who will use it?; two, what is the base style guide in use?; and three, how complicated is it?

So, will I alone be referencing this style guide (and perhaps the author), or will PR and blogging staff and other writers be referencing it? Will it be presented in alphabetical order and cross-referenced (as with AP style)? CMOS and APA each have their own numbering systems by category pertinent to the subject areas that frequently utilize them; perhaps I can design mine in this way or use one of their sets of categories. Alternatively, could I set it up as a table or a chart? What it comes down to is that some sort of logical order needs to be applied if anyone besides the editor may need to use it.

For a bucket-list self-publishing memoirist, where really the style is only for my reference, I figure I'm just fine with a page of handwritten notes. For something a bit more formal, a word processing program might be the easiest place to create a simple style guide. For an even more formal template, the AP website has a feature where a user can create a *custom style book*, and CMOS Online has a similar feature for making a *style sheet*. They vary in their strategy—no doubt particular to the field for which they are designed. On CMOS Online, you can create as many style sheets as you have projects and clients. I like to use this feature because in addition to noting house style specs, I can copy and paste frequently referenced CMOS rules right there and have what is, in essence, a cheat sheet for myself.

For Scenario #1, because Aimee is bulding a brand, it might be best to create a somewhat formal list indicating the quirky elements that should remain consistent in order to uphold her unique brand. It might make sense to alphabetize the entries for ease of use. Perhaps it would look something like Figure iii.

For Scenario #2, Marla will need a more formal document, which might be created in a Google Doc or in an online style guide that can be easily passed on to a new generation of staff. Since we are using CMOS, categorical references to that style guide may make it easier to keep track. And to make it easier for the next editors, who may not be as familiar with CMOS, I can include references to commonly encountered CMOS rules that are often broken and should be consistently applied. See Figure iv.

For Scenario #3, a table or figure might make the most sense for The Cookwell Team. Chefs might like annotated recipes or easy charts. See Figure v.

5. Apply

After we have established the style guide that best suits the writer and their rhetorical situation, we copyedit the manuscript referencing these

What's Your Style?

Figure iii. Alphabetical style guide

Aimee's Style Guidelines
PERTAINING TO: Inspiration book #1 and subsequent booklets, press releases, website and blog content, and social media outreach, when applicable.

accommodate (commonly misspelled)
achieve (commonly misspelled)
acquire (commonly misspelled)
ACT: use all caps when used emphatically
AM (as a reference to ante meridian time, not as the -to be verb. As a to-be verb, should be lowercase).
apostrophes: ending in -s and plural possessive, use s' or es'. No extra -s after apostrophe
Beauty: capitalized first letter only if used in a catch phrase or as a proper noun
Beauty Beyond Belief: Title case as catch phrase.
BUILD: all caps when used emphatically
CAPITALIZATION:
- catch-phrases should be title capped like this: Prepare, Practice and be Passionate; Beauty Beyond Belief; Confidence is Beautiful;
- For headlines in the online event calendar, use headline-style capitalization; capitalize all major words in the headline, including prepositions of four letters or more.
- use ALL CAPS for certain high energy verbs when used emphatically. For instance: CULTIVATE, ACT, DARE, BUILD;
- use lowercase (except at the start of sentences): am, commit, garden, life, confidence, finally
- Twitter is capitalized as a proper noun, but tweet as a verb is not.

commit: lowercase unless at the start of a sentence
competition (commonly misspelled)
confidence: do not capitalize for emphasis.
Confidence is Beautiful: Title case as catch phrase
convenience (commonly misspelled)
CULTIVATE: use all caps when used emphatically
DASHES: See CMOS 6.78-6.81. No space on either side of em dash or en dash.
DATES: Month Day, Year. or MO/DA/YEAR. Time zones, where needed, are usually given in parentheses
dictionary: Use *Merriam-Webster's Collegiate Dictionary*, online.
disappoint (commonly misspelled)
discipline (commonly misspelled)
ebook: no hyphen
email: no hyphen, lower-case e.
finally: do not capitalize for emphasis.
gender: use "they" as singular gender neutral over any he/she construction.
headlines: For headlines in the all major words in the headline,
healthcare: one word
he/she: see gender
hyperlink:
- Always include hyperlink
- Hide links behind text.
- When writing out links in

hyphen
- after a hyphen in a compound, use a lowercase letter
- An abbreviated compound is treated as a single word, so a hyphen, not an en dash, is used in such phrases as "US-Canadian relations."
- A hyphen is used to separate numbers that are not inclusive, such as telephone numbers

internet: lowercase
italics: use italics for words in languages other than English and other unfamiliar terms (over quotation marks) on the first occurrence.
link: see hyperlink
login: as a noun/adjective
log in: as a verb
logout: as a noun/adjective
log out as a verb
nonprofit: no hyphen
nontraditional: no hyphen
numbers:
- spell out single digit numbers: one, two, three; and other numbers if they start a sentence, or preferably, revise the sentence so it doesn't start with a number.
- spell out ordinal numbers: first, second, third, fifth.

online: no hyphen
PM
SOCIAL MEDIA:
- Emphasize preservation of voice of the writer and tone of the piece while conforming as much as possible to Standard American Written English rules. Don't sweat it.
- Be committed to eliminating biased or discriminatory language.
- *They* is preferable to indicate the singular gender neutral.

SPECIAL TERMINOLOGY/USAGE LISTING
Twitter/tweet: the name of the site/app is a proper noun therefore capitalized, the action performed is lowercase. One who tweets on Twitter is a tweeter.
unfamiliar terms: first use of a word in a language other than English is italicized, subsequent mentions are not. See italics.
web addresses: Omit http:// and www. before an address, e.g., the-efa.org. Hyperlinks should always be included.

> **Marla's Magazine Style Guide**
>
> *Editors: Be alert for these frequently encountered style issues. We use the* **Chicago Manual of Style** *as our house style guide and this is intended to supplement, not replace, CMOS. The most common style fixes we require are listed here. Also, where there is ambiguity, we have adopted the rules listed here. (Numbers correspond CMOS Table of Contents)*
>
> **1. Formatting:** See manuscript prep document titled   (appendix A)
>
> **5.220: Good usage versus common usage**
> Edit towards to toward (no –s)
> Use til no apostrophe (not 'til or till as short word for until)
> Watch for commonly confused words. Like poring vs pouring. A good, yet incomplete list of these words can be found here:
> http://www.stlcc.edu/Student_Resources/Academic_Resources/Writing_Resources/Grammar_Handouts/commonly_confused_words.pdf
>
> **5.6 Wine varieties: Capitalize.**
> http://www.delongwine.com/blogs/de-long-wine-moment/14610331-should-grape-varieties-be-capitalized
>
> **6. Punctuation in relation to closing quotation marks**
> Commas and periods always go inside closing quotation marks.
> Semicolons & colons come after a closing quotation mark.
> Colons and semicolons—unlike periods and commas—follow closing quotation marks; question marks and exclamation points follow closing quotation marks unless they belong within the quoted matter. (This rule applies the logic that is often absent from the US style described in 6.9.) See also table 6.1.
>
> **6.59-6.61 Capitalization following colon**
> Capitalize independent clause following a colon and lowercase following semicolon.
>
> **6.82 Em dashes instead of commas, parentheses, or colons**
> To avoid confusion, the em dash should never be used within or immediately following another element set off by an em dash (or pair of em dashes). Use parentheses or commas instead.
>
> **7.55 "Scare quotes"** Edit them out (eliminate) when possible.
> Don't ever use single quote marks as scare quotes, or as a way to indicate something is so-called. If this is required, use regular double quote marks (unless it is inside someone's direct quote).
>
> **7.85 Hyphen guidelines**
> nonfiction: no hyphen
> http://www.chicagomanualofstyle.org/16/images/ch07_tab01.pdf
>
> | age terms | a three-year-old
a five-year-old child
a fifty-five-year-old woman
a group of eight- to ten-year-olds | Hyphenated in both noun and adjective forms (except as in the last two examples); note the space after the first hyphen in the fourth example (see 7.84). The examples apply equally to ages expressed as numerals. |
> |---|---|---|
>
> **8. Names and Terms**

Figure iv. CMOS-based style sheet

guidelines as often as we need to during our last passes through it. This is where the Find feature in Microsoft Word becomes my best friend. I can find all instances where *tbsp* appears in the cookbook and replace it manually with either *T* (in an ingredient list) or *tablespoon* (in instructions). I can use Find and Replace when there is something more universal, like replacing the word *degree* with the symbol °; or all instances where an em dash appears with a space on each side, replacing it with an em dash, no spaces. Similarly, I can find all the times the writer spelled the name Jeffry and fix it to become Jeffrey. Not all changes can be incorporated

What's Your Style?

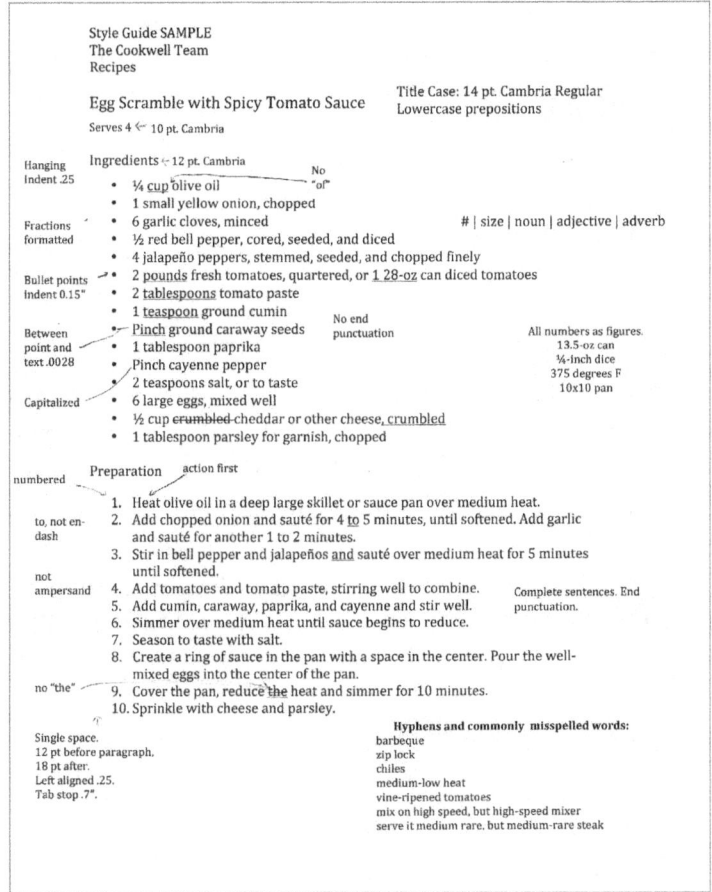

Figure v. Annotated image style sheet

this way, but when they can, it sure is nice. A great sense of satisfaction can be gained during this process—as we see the changes implemented, the consistency established, and the content shining through.

In *The Subversive Copy Editor*, Saller writes:

> The midwife works with a laboring woman to produce a healthy child. A seamstress or tailor finishes the couturier's garment until it's a perfect, flattering fit. Carpenters and masons execute an architect's vision and take pride in a safe and well functioning

building. What we all have in common is our wish to cooperate—not compete—with the originators of our material, and we share a satisfaction and sense of accomplishment when everything is going well.[15]

Quite.

6. Adjust and Refine

Occasionally, feedback from a reader will cause us to look again at the style we implemented. Someone will be distracted or confused by a lack of hyphenation or put off by formatting. It is acceptable to revisit. But make sure to go back and revisit the entire document, not just a single chapter or incident.

Keep your mind as open as your eyes and you might actually find you enjoy building a custom style for your client or publication. Editing is not policing—it can be creative and fun.

Notes

1. Norm Goldstein, ed., *The Associated Press Stylebook and Libel Manual.* (Reading, Massachusetts: Addison-Wesley, 1998).

2. Joseph Gibaldi, *MLA Handbook for Writers of Research Papers*, 6th ed. (New York: The Modern Language Association of America, 2003).

3. *Publication Manual of the American Psychological Association*, 5th ed. (Washington, DC: American Psychological Association, 2001).

4. "Style." *AMA Manual of Style: A Guide for Authors and Editors*, 11th ed. (Oxford University Press Online, 2009.

5. Goldstein, *The Associated Press Stylebook.*

6. "The History of the Chicago Manual of Style." The Chicago Manual of Style Online. Accessed April 20, 2017.

7. Katharine O'Moore-Klopf, "Style Sheets." KOK Edit online. Accessed December 3, 2020. http://kokedit.com/library_stylesheets.php.

8. Cheryl Murphy, EFA Discussion List, Message #125170, May 16, 2016.

9. Carol Fisher Saller, *The Subversive Copy Editor: Advice from Chicago*, 2nd ed. (Chicago: The University of Chicago Press, 2016), xvii.

10. Ethan Sproat et al., "Elements of Rhetorical Situations." Purdue Online Writing Lab. Last modified April 27, 2012. Accessed December 3, 2020. https://owl.purdue.edu/owl/general_writing/academic_writing/rhetorical_situation/elements_of_rhetorical_situations.html.

11. QQAdmin1, "Should I Use The Chicago Manual of Style for my Book?" blog post on November 18, 2008. WritersDigest.com. Accessed December 3, 2020. http://www.writersdigest.com/editor-blogs/questions-and-quandaries/dealing-with-editors/should-i-use-the-chicago-manual-of-style-for-my-book.

12. https://consciousstyleguide.com/about/.

13. Laurel Ferejohn, "Editing: A Fear-Free Zone." Laurel Ferejohn online. Accessed December 3, 2020. http://laurelferejohn.com/laurelferejohn/.

14. Saller, *Subversive Copy Editor*, 14.

15. Saller, xix.

About the Editorial Freelancers Association (EFA)

Celebrating 50 Years!
Dedicated to the Education and Growth
of Editorial Freelancers

The EFA is a national not-for-profit — 501(c)6 — organization, headquartered in New York City, run by member volunteers, all of whom are also freelancers. The EFA's members, experienced in a wide range of professional skills, live and work all across the United States and in other countries.

A pioneer in organizing freelancers into a network for mutual support and advancement, the EFA is now recognized throughout the publishing industry as the source for professional editorial assistance.

We welcome people of every race, color, culture, religion or no religion, gender identity, gender expression, age, national or ethnic origin, ancestry, citizenship, education, ability, health, neurotype, marital/parental status, socioeconomic background, sexual orientation, and/or military status. We are nothing without our members, and encourage everyone to volunteer and to participate in our community.

The EFA sells a variety of specialized booklets, not unlike this one, on topics of interest to editorial freelancers at the-efa.org.

The EFA hosts online, asynchronous courses, real-time webinars, and on-demand recorded webinars designed especially for freelance editors, writers, and other editorial specialists around the world. You can learn more about our Education Program at the-efa.org.

To learn about these and other EFA offerings, visit the-efa.org and join us on social media:

Twitter: @EFAFreelancers
Instagram: @efa_editors
Facebook: editorialfreelancersassociation
LinkedIn: editorial-freelancers

www.ingramcontent.com/pod-product-compliance
Lightning Source LLC
Chambersburg PA
CBHW071551080526
44588CB00011B/1865